ANIMAL PLANET

DINOSAURS!

LORI STEIN

DINOSAURS!

Published by Liberty Street,
an imprint of Time Inc. Books
225 Liberty Street
New York, New York 10281

LIBERTY
STREET

LIBERTY STREET is a trademark of Time Inc.

ISBN 10: 1-61893-186-5
ISBN 13: 978-1-61893-186-3

First edition, 2016

1 QGT 16

10 9 8 7 6 5 4 3 2 1

Some of the content in this book was originally published in *Discovery Dinopedia: The Complete Guide to Everything Dinosaur.*

Produced by Scout Books & Media Inc

Time Inc. Books products may be purchased for business or promotional use. For information on bulk purchases, please contact Christi Crowley in the Special Sales Department at (845) 895-9858.

To order Time Inc. Books Collector's Editions, please call (800) 327-6388, Monday through Friday, 7 a.m.–9 p.m., Central Time.

We welcome your comments and suggestions about Time Inc. Books. Please write to us at: Time Inc. Books, Attention: Book Editors, P.O. Box 62310, Tampa, Florida 33662–2310.

timeincbooks.com

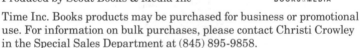

Dinosaur names are often long and hard to pronounce. The first time a dinosaur name is used, it appears in **bold**. You can find a guide to pronouncing all the dinosaur names in the book on page 110.

CONTENTS

DINO TIME! The Age of Dinosaurs lasted from 252 million to 66 million years ago. That's about 186 million years.

CHAPTER 1

THE AGE OF DINOSAURS

For about 186 million years, a group of amazing creatures roamed our planet. This was the Age of Dinosaurs. There were thousands of different types of dinosaurs. They lived, ate, fought, and raised families. Some were huge—among the largest animals ever to live on Earth. Others were small. Fast or slow, fierce or gentle, they lived successfully for millions of years. They vanished about 66 million years ago. But dinosaurs left evidence that we can study to learn about them.

Dinosaurs lived in a world that is very different from Earth today. Our planet is about 4.6 billion years old. During the first few billion years, Earth's air had little oxygen. There was almost no life on the planet. Over time, the air became easier to breathe and small creatures appeared. The earliest known creatures lived in water. Some evolved to live on land. Then, dinosaurs appeared.

When dinosaurs became extinct (died out), their fossils remained. What is a fossil? Fossils can form when a creature dies in a place with the right amount of water and silt (bits of sand or clay in water). If this mixture buries the bones quickly, the skin and flesh rot away. The silt settles on the bones. This protects and preserves them. Bones can stay undisturbed this way for millions of years.

Scientists also learn a lot from coprolites (fossilized dinosaur poop), dinosaur eggs and nests, and tracks that were made by dinosaur feet. Sometimes,

WHAT IS EVOLUTION?

Evolution explains how living things change over time. Some dinosaurs were born with features that made them better able to survive. A dinosaur with a useful new feature passed that feature on to its babies. After thousands of years, dinosaurs without that feature died out.

in a place where a dinosaur rested or died, an outline of its body was left behind. These are ways we learn about dinosaurs and their world.

People have been discovering dinosaur bones for thousands of years. At first no one knew what they were. Some thought they might be the bones of dragons or giants. About 200 years ago, people began to recognize them as the bones of very large animals.

Scientists divide dinosaurs into two orders. The saurischian (lizard-hipped) and ornithischian (bird-hipped). These orders are divided again into groups. Dinosaurs in each group share common features.

One group in the

saurischian order, called theropods, walked on two feet. They were the only dinosaurs that were carnivores— they ate meat. Theropods range from huge predators, such as *Tyrannosaurus rex,* which hunted other animals, to small, birdlike creatures such as *Troodon*.

Troodon

Brachiosaurus

The sauropod group were also saurischians. They walked on four legs and were herbivores. They ate plants. Sauropods include ***Brachiosaurus*** and ***Apatosaurus***. These dinosaurs grew very large and moved slowly. They had small heads and brains.

The ornithischian order of dinosaurs includes thyreophorans, ornithopods, and marginocephalians. Thyreophorans were large and heavy. They had bony plates on their bodies. ***Stegosaurus*** and

Ankylosaurus

Ankylosaurus are two types. They walked on four legs and ate plants.

Hadrosaurus

The dinosaurs in the ornithopod group also ate plants. They switched from walking on four legs when they were looking for food to running on two legs to escape a predator. *Iguanodon* and *Hadrosaurus* are in this group.

The maginocephalian group includes dinosaurs with pointed horns, such as *Triceratops*. Dinosaurs such as *Stegoceras* belong in this group, too. They all walked on four legs and ate plants.

Triceratops

WE'VE GOT YOUR SIZE

People think of dinosaurs as huge animals. Some of them were the largest to ever walk on land. But dinosaurs came in every size. The largest was as tall as a four-story building. The smallest was the size of a chicken. Here's how six popular dinos stack up.

A

B

Humans average 5.5 feet in height

Length from tip of snout to tip of tail

A Over 40 feet: *Brachiosaurus*

B 30–40 feet: *Yangchuanosaurus*

C 20–30 feet: *Stegosaurus*

WHAT MAKES A DINOSAUR A DINOSAUR?

HARD AND SOFT PALATE The palate is the roof of the mouth. The shape of dinosaurs' palates allowed the animals to eat and breathe at the same time.

HOLES IN THE HEAD Dinosaur skulls had three pairs of openings, not counting the eyes and nostrils.

HOLE IN THE HIP Every dinosaur had a hole through each hip socket.

STOOD UPRIGHT Whether they walked on two or four legs, dinosaurs stood upright. Their legs were directly beneath their bodies.

D 10–20 feet: *Zuniceratops*

E 5–10 feet: *Deinonychus*

F Under 5 feet: *Archaeopteryx*

Experts divide time on our planet into long spans called eras. There are four eras: Precambrian, Paleozoic, Mesozoic, and Cenozoic. Dinosaurs lived during the Mesozoic Era. Within this era, there are three periods of time. These periods mark when different dinosaurs lived and died out.

During the Triassic Period (252 million to 201 million years ago), the first dinosaurs appeared in what is now South America. They were mostly small carnivores. Triassic dinosaurs include *Coelophysis*, *Eoraptor*, and *Herrerasaurus*.

The Jurassic Period (201 million to 144 million years ago), was a time

when huge dinosaurs ruled the world. There were small furry animals. Flowering plants became food for herbivores. Some Jurassic dinosaurs are **Dilophosaurus**, **Massospondylus**, **Dryosaurus**, **Allosaurus**, *Apatosaurus*, **Diplodocus**, and *Stegosaurus*.

Dinosaurs continued to dominate in the Cretaceous Period (144 million to 66 million years ago). Cretaceous dinosaurs include *Deinonychus*, **Psittacosaurus**, **Parasaurolophus**, *Triceratops*, and *Tyrannosaurus rex*.

Then, 66 million years ago, dinosaurs became extinct. No one knows exactly why. It was probably because a huge asteroid hit Earth.

GIVING CHASE! *T. rex* could run on two feet to chase prey. This one is after a **Velociraptor**.

WHEN "BEAST FEET" WALKED THE EARTH

Theropods lived throughout the entire Age of Dinosaurs. The earliest known dinosaurs were theropods, and theropods were still around when the dinosaurs vanished 66 million years ago. The name *theropod* comes from two Greek words that mean "beast feet." When the largest theropods stomped around, the ground trembled. Smaller animals would have run away.

Many theropods had birdlike bodies

with hollow bones. This made them light and fast. Others, including *Tyrannosaurus rex*, were heavy and slow. All of them had big, sharp teeth for eating meat. They had large eyes and large brains that helped them hunt and avoid attacks.

Paleontologists have found 267 kinds of theropods. Their fossils have been found everywhere in the world.

Theropods came in many different sizes, from less than 3 feet to more than 45 feet long. Some had long, curving necks, and tails and jaws shaped like a crocodile's. Others had shorter necks, tails, and snouts. They all walked on two feet, ate meat, and had hollow bones.

Early theropods were smaller and less fierce

than the ones that came later. But they still had very sharp teeth and claws, strong legs, and hollow bones that made them light enough to run quickly. These animals include *Herrerasaurus* and **Tawa**, which lived during the Late Triassic Period.

Over millions of years, dinosaurs became bigger and deadlier. Small changes in their bodies, such as sharper claws and stronger tails,

WHICH DINOSAURS WERE THE SMARTEST?

Paleontologists think *Troodon* was as smart as modern raptors, such as eagles and hawks. *Deinonychus* was also intelligent, and probably hunted in groups.

made them better predators. Some of the most famous meat eaters, such as *Allosaurus*, **Spinosaurus**, and **Carcharodontosaurus**, were the top predators of their time. They ate other animals, but no other animals ate them! They were also among the biggest theropods that ever lived.

Allosaurus had a special jaw joint so it could open its mouth super wide and hold huge chunks of flesh. It also had bony ridges over each eye that may have worked like sunshades.

Spinosaurus had powerful jaws like a crocodile's,

Allosaurus

with sharp teeth and a 6-foot-high, fan-shaped sail on its back. Scientists think it

Spinosaurus

may have used the sail to control its temperature by absorbing or releasing body heat. Or it may have used it to signal other dinosaurs.

Carcharodontosaurus had a massive body and tail. Its head was 5 feet long and its sharp teeth were 8 inches long. It was bigger than *Tyrannosaurus rex*.

From the Late Jurassic Period to the Late Cretaceous Period, many new dinosaurs appeared. Although the dinosaurs in this group looked different from one another, they all had stiff tails and feathers of some sort. Some of them (such as ***Ornithomimus***) became more like birds. Others (such as *Tyrannosaurus rex*) became bigger and deadlier. They were called tyrant dinosaurs. A tyrant is a creature that uses power to control weaker creatures.

Many kinds of tyrant dinosaurs lived in North America and Asia at the end of the Cretaceous Period. Most of the tyrant dinosaurs were the biggest and strongest animals in their environment. They fought and ate other animals.

They had massive skulls, sharp teeth, small arms, and big tails, which helped them balance. One of the last groups of theropods were near-raptors, which looked a lot like birds. They are closely

TYRANT TEETH

Tyrant dinosaurs had lots of big, sharp teeth. As many as 70 teeth lined their jaws and gave them a frightening appearance. Their teeth had tiny cracks, but these cracks didn't make them weaker. The cracks helped distribute pressure along the jaws. This meant the tyrants could bite with tremendous force without breaking their teeth.

related to predator birds, such as eagles and hawks. The near-raptor dinosaurs were covered with feathers. Their arm bones were similar to wing bones.

Velociraptor

Many near-raptors ate plants. They probably chopped them off with their claws and beaked jaws.

Most near-raptors were less than 10 feet tall. *Therizinosaurus* was an exception. At almost 40 feet long, it was one of the biggest theropods. Many near-raptors, such as *Oviraptor*, were found in Asia, and some have been found in North and South America. *Deinonychus* and *Velociraptor* were also birdlike dinosaurs. They were vicious and may have hunted in packs.

FACT FILE: FOSSIL STORIES

Fossils can reveal fascinating stories about how dinosaurs lived and died.

Ghost Ranch is an area in New Mexico where many dinosaur fossils have been found. Hundreds of *Coelophysis* skeletons were discovered in huge, tangled piles. In the Triassic Period, this area was located near the Equator. Scientists think heavy rains could have caused flash floods that drowned a whole pack of these dinosaurs.

Coelophysis

Big Al

When a team of paleontologists found a nearly complete *Allosaurus* skeleton in Wyoming in 1991, at first they thought it was an adult dinosaur. But when they looked closer, they realized it was probably an adolescent. The bones told the story of the difficult life this young dinosaur had. It had lost limbs, broken ribs and other bones, and suffered infections. The scientists named the skeleton "Big Al" and wrote its life story. Later, a television show called *The Ballad of Big Al* showed its life from birth to death.

CRUNCH THIS! *T. rex*'s bite was the strongest of any animal that ever lived.

CHAPTER
3

T. REX: THE KING OF DINOSAURS

Tyrannosaurus rex means "tyrant lizard king," and this dinosaur lived up to its name. It was a powerful and vicious ruler of the planet. *T. rex* was a theropod dinosaur, which means it walked on two feet and ate meat. It was a top predator. Its sharp teeth and powerful 4-foot-long jaw could crunch through bone and rip apart flesh. *T. rex* wasn't the largest dinosaur, but it was the biggest carnivore of its day. It grew up to 40 feet long and weighed up to 15,000 pounds. That's as long as a school bus and as heavy as nine polar bears.

T. rex was one of the last dinosaurs to appear, about 2 million years before all dinosaurs became extinct. Like other theropods, *T. rex* had an enormous skull, strong teeth and claws, small arms, and a big tail. *T. rex*'s awesome body and physical abilities made it the most deadly dinosaur of its day.

It had powerful back legs and could run in an upright position. The sharp claws on its small hands and big feet could catch, hold, and rip apart prey (animals to eat). Its short arms would not have helped it attack other dinosaurs. But some experts think those arms were very strong. They were used to grip live prey, while the jaws worked on tearing flesh.

Good vision allowed *T. rex* to spot prey or other animals looking to fight over something (maybe a mate or food). It had deep eye sockets and eyes pointing straight ahead. These gave *T. rex* better

DID ANYONE BATTLE T. REX?

T. rex didn't have an easy life. It lived in a dino-eat-dino world. Fossils show that *T. rex* was gored by horned dinosaurs that were defending themselves. It also lost limbs in fights and was sometimes attacked by other *T. rexes*.

PINOCCHIO REX

NOSE FOR NEWS

In the spring of 2014, paleontologists in China found a smaller cousin of *T. rex* that had a long snout. They officially named it **Qianzhousaurus**, but commonly call it "Pinocchio rex" after its impressive nose. It's a theropod *Tyrannosaurus* like *T. rex*. It was about 29 feet long—including its super long snout.

depth perception than dinosaurs with eyes pointing to the sides, so it could see how far away something was. *T. rex* had much bigger eyes than a human, so its vision was probably better than ours.

By examining the size of its nose, scientists can tell that *T. rex* had the best sense of smell of any dinosaur.

It could find something to eat by smelling it from far away.

T. rex's teeth were 8 to 9 inches long. There were more than 50 of them in its massive jaws. Each tooth was cone-shaped, curved, and strong enough to crunch through bones. The teeth were not super sharp. Instead, they were

ALWAYS A HUNTER?

In 2013, scientists found a *T. rex* tooth in a fossil of a duckbilled dinosaur's tailbone. This proves that *T. rex* hunted and killed its food. But some paleontologists think *T. rex* was also a scavenger. It might have looked for dead animals to eat instead of always killing live ones. Finding and killing a big dinosaur, such as *Triceratops*, could have fed a *T. rex* for several weeks. But eating a dead animal it found would have taken less energy and been less dangerous.

T. rex used its strong bite to kill and eat prey.

solid and could chomp down on animals of any size.

T. rex's bite was three times as strong as a great white shark's or a crocodile's, and 60 times as strong as a human's. It had the strongest bite of any animal that ever lived. The bite was strong because its teeth were big and solid. Plus, its skull and jaws were enormous, and it could open its mouth very wide.

T. rex fossils are usually found alone. This means they probably were loners and didn't hunt in packs.

How smart was *T. rex*? Scientists measure a dinosaur's intelligence by comparing the size of its brain to the size of its body. By that measurement, *T. rex* is one of the smartest dinosaurs.

FACT FILE: A DINOSAUR NAMED SUE

The largest, best-preserved, and most complete *Tyrannosaurus rex* skeleton ever discovered is nicknamed "Sue." Sue's skeleton was found in the Badlands of South Dakota. It has been put together, and now is on display in the Field Museum in Chicago.

This remarkable find even includes the tiny bones of the inner ear, which have rarely been found with T. rex skeletons. By studying the bones in Sue's skull that were around its brain, scientists made a fascinating discovery: A large part of Sue's brain was used to recognize smells.

Since the exhibit opened in May 2000, more than 16 million people have visited Sue. So far, no one knows whether Sue was male or female. The skeleton was named for the paleontologist who discovered it, Sue Hendrickson.

Sue's discovery was a happy accident. Several researchers were ready to drive home from a field trip when their car got a flat tire. Most of the group went to a nearby town to have the tire repaired. But Sue Hendrickson decided to stay behind and look around a site that the group hadn't explored. She looked up from the base of a cliff and saw a few bones stuck in the rocks about 8 feet above her head. The bones were big enough to go have a look.

Sue is more than 42 feet long.
The bones weigh 3,922 pounds.

GROWTH CURVE! An *Argentinosaurus* egg was the size of a coconut. It grew 25,000 times its hatchling size to become an adult.

CHAPTER 4

BABIES, FAMILIES, AND HERDS

ow did dinosaurs begin their lives? Even the biggest, deadliest dinosaur started out as a baby hatched from an egg. Many types of dinosaurs went through a time where they needed their parents to take care of them, like human babies do. Others were able to care for themselves right after they were born. From fossils, scientists have learned a great deal about how dinosaur babies were born and how they grew up.

Dinosaurs had a special way of finding mates and having babies. For example, an *Eoraptor* male built a nest and showed it to a female. A good nest was important for having a family. Some experts think this was one of the ways to attract a mate. Later, the female laid eggs in the nest. Dinosaurs laid many eggs at a time.

Some dinosaurs, such as **Gigantoraptor**, sat on their nests. This is called brooding. It's a way to keep eggs warm at night and cool during the day. This steady, even source of heat helped the eggs develop properly. Modern birds, which are closely related to dinosaurs, also brood. Bigger dinosaurs, too heavy to sit on their eggs, may have covered them with plants to keep them warm.

Finally, the eggs cracked open. What happened to the baby dinosaurs after they hatched from their shells? Many dinosaur parents took care of their babies. Young dinosaurs often stayed in their nests for a few months or even longer. And even after they left the nest, some dinosaurs hung around with their siblings.

Many young dinosaurs learned how to find food by hunting or foraging (finding plant food) with their parents. The parents showed their babies how to look for food, and protected them when predators came near.

Some fossils of young dinosaurs were found near both male and female adults. This might mean dinosaur fathers stayed around to care for their young. In Cody, Wyoming, 20 adult and young ***Drinker*** dinosaurs were found together in a hole, with the adults on top of the children. Scientists think the parents pushed their children into the hole to escape a predator.

Dinosaurs grew slowly for the first few years of their lives—and then grew very large, very fast. By the time it reached the age of ten, a *Tyrannosaurus rex* weighed about 1,000 pounds. In the next few years, it grew 1,000 pounds each year. When it reached its adult weight of 12,000 pounds, it stopped growing. Different kinds of

FACT FILE: NESTING NOTES

For many years, scientists thought dinosaurs hatched from eggs, but were not sure. How did they find out for sure? In 1978, paleontologist Jack Horner discovered some fossilized dinosaur nests, eggshells, and embryos in Montana. From this important find, we learned how dinosaurs made their nests, cared for their eggs, and fed their babies after they were hatched.

Model of a Maiasaura nest

dinosaurs grew up in different ways. Some, such as *Argentinosaurus*, were able to take care of themselves as soon as they were born. They learned to move around, find food, and avoid being attacked.

Some dinosaurs lived in groups called herds. They hunted, ate, and traveled together. Many animals live in herds today, including elephants, antelopes, and buffalo.

Paleontologists believe dinosaurs that lived in herds behaved the way modern herd animals do. It's possible there were leaders, followers, and battles for position. Dinosaur nests have been found grouped together. Giving birth was sometimes part of herd life. Protecting young, sick, and old members from attack was another herd activity.

Argentinosaurus herd

EASY GLIDER *Archaeopteryx* was covered with feathers. They were not spaced the right way for strong, fast flight. This means it probably did more gliding than flying.

LOOK! UP IN THE SKY!

Where did modern birds come from? At one time, scientists believed that they came from large flying reptiles called pterosaurs. Then they thought a winged theropod dinosaur might be the first bird. But many other theropod dinosaurs had birdlike features and did not fly. Experts now agree that modern birds evolved from these theropod dinosaurs. There's much more still to discover about how dinosaurs evolved into flying animals.

In 1861, a small animal that looked like a raven was discovered in a fossil bed in Germany. This new creature was called *Archaeopteryx*. Was it a bird or a dinosaur? Paleontologists have debated this question for a long time. Some experts said *Archaeopteryx* was the first bird. It had wings and feathers, and probably could fly. Most experts agree that *Archaeopteryx* was a link between dinosaurs and birds. It was part dinosaur and part bird.

IN YOUR NEWSFEED

DINOS WITH WINGS

In 2015, scientists in China discovered a well-preserved fossil of a close relative of *Velociraptor*. They named it **Zhenyuanlong suni**. It had very short arms, so it probably could not fly. But the fossil showed that it had long tail feathers and wings.

The ancestors of birds included *Deinonychus*, *Oviraptor*, and *Velociraptor*. These smart carnivores walked on two legs, like birds. Their arms were short, but the bones in them were similar to wings. They had feathers but did not fly. At some point, their bird descendants lifted off the ground. How that happened is still a mystery.

SIMILAR TRAITS

Dinosaurs had feathers! They first appeared on theropods about 150 million years ago. Pretty feathers might have helped attract a mate.

Some dinosaurs, such as *Velociraptor*, had sharp claws. These helped catch and hold prey while eating.

Theropods walked on two legs. So do birds. In fact, since birds evolved from theropod dinosaurs, you can call them living dinosaurs.

WHAT WERE THEY?

Pterosaurs were large flying reptiles that lived during the Age of Dinosaurs. But they weren't dinosaurs. Until about 50 years ago, some scientists believed birds evolved from pterosaurs or a close relative. But now all agree that they evolved from theropod dinosaurs.

Quetzalcoatlus

Anhanguera was a pterosaur from the Early Cretaceous Period. It had a wingspan of 15 feet. Its legs were weak. It probably spent very little time on the ground. *Quetzalcoatlus* was a pterosaur from the Late Cretaceous Period. It had the largest wingspan—around 36 feet—of any known animal. It probably pushed off with both front and back legs. Its wings worked like sails on a boat.

But pterosaurs did not have feathers. Their skeletons do not resemble the skeletons of modern birds. When scientists compared bird skeletons to dinosaur fossils, they discovered something surprising: Birds evolved from fast theropod dinosaurs called near-raptors and paravians.

BIG AND TALL *Brachiosaurus* means "arm lizard." Its arms were longer than its legs.

GENTLE GIANTS

auropods were huge plant-eating
dinosaurs. The name sauropod
comes from a Greek word
meaning "lizard feet." Most had similar
features: an enormous body, four thick
legs, and lizardlike feet with claws.
Their big size helped them scare away
predators. Big stomachs gave them
extra storage space for food. There are
198 known sauropods—about ten times
as many as theropods. Sauropod fossils
have been found on all seven continents.

The first sauropods appeared in the Late Triassic Period, more than 200 million years ago. Some of the earliest ones ate meat and walked on two legs. Early sauropods were large compared to other animals of the time. But they were smaller than the giants that followed.

Eoraptor is one of the earliest dinosaurs identified as a sauropod. It was small, weighed about 20 pounds, and ate meat. *Massospondylus* could walk on both two and four feet. It was 13 to 20 feet long and weighed about 300 pounds. It was an omnivore. It ate both meat and plants.

Vulcanodon, an herbivore, lived in the Early Jurassic Period, about 200 million to 180 million years ago. It walked on

four feet and weighed about
8,000 pounds. That's as much
as two cars.

Over millions of years, the earliest
sauropods evolved into gigantic
dinosaurs—the largest animals that
ever walked on land. As they grew

Eoraptors

BIG BABIES

HIGH TECH DATA

Scientists are using modern equipment like CT scanners and computer models to understand how sauropods grew so big. They found that the babies grew super fast. Hatchlings went from 7 pounds to 80 pounds in about eight weeks.

bigger, they needed to walk on all four legs to support their weight. Their diet shifted to only plants.

By the Middle Jurassic Period, starting around 180 million years ago, they had super long necks and tails, and small heads. There were big nostrils on the tops of their heads.

Two of the most famous sauropods from the Middle Jurassic Period are **Camarasaurus** and *Brachiosaurus. Camarasaurus* had a short neck and tail, and weighed up to 95,000 pounds. That's as much as a big helicopter. Fossilized tracks show that *Camarasaurus* traveled in herds and covered long distances. The herds probably moved on when food or water became scarce.

Brachiosaurus's arms were longer than its legs by more than a foot. (*Brachia* means "arms.") This huge dinosaur walked on all four limbs, so its shoulders and neck were higher than its back. It would have been able to reach the tops of the trees without stretching its long neck.

A replica of a titanosaur, one of the largest dinosaurs ever discovered

Titanosaurs were a group of very large dinosaurs that appeared in the Cretaceous Period. (*Titan* means "giant.") They lived until dinosaurs disappeared 66 million years ago. There may have been more than 100 different types of dinosaurs in this group. They include some of the largest dinosaurs ever discovered.

One of the titanosaurs, *Argentinosaurus*, was about 115 feet long and weighed more than 146,000 pounds. An *Argentinosaurus* egg was the size of a coconut. A baby grew 25,000 times its hatchling size to become an adult.

Whiptail dinosaurs had a very long neck, a whiplike tail, and a huge body with a big belly on short legs. Some of the biggest and most well-known dinosaurs were in the whiptail group, including *Apatosaurus* and *Diplodocus*. They grew to more than 100 feet long and had some of longest necks and tails of all animals.

***Apatosaurus* was one of the largest** animals to ever live on land. It is also one of the most popular dinosaurs of all time. It was very strong and heavily built. Its vertebrae (the bones in its spine) were arranged so it could hold its tail above the ground to maintain balance.

Its name means "deceptive lizard." That means it seems to be something it is not. When it was first discovered, experts found that some of its bones were similar to those of reptiles. But they determined that *Apatosaurus* was really a dinosaur.

For about 100 years, *Apatosaurus* was called ***Brontosaurus***. Why was the name changed? Fossil hunter O.C. Marsh discovered two dinosaur skeletons a long time ago. He named the first one *Apatosaurus* and the second one *Brontosaurus*. Neither skeleton had its head attached. (Sauropod skulls are lightly attached to their bodies and often rolled away.)

For a while scientists thought they had two different dinosaurs. Later, paleontologists studying the bones realized that they were the same animal. The first name, *Apatosaurus*, is the one that stuck.

Apatosaurus skull

BODY OF THE BEAST

Experts have a good idea about how
dinosaur bones fit together because
some full skeletons have been found.
This *T. rex* model is one example.

TAIL was long
and heavy.

LIZARD-HIPPED

LEGS AND FEET
were built for
running.

What *T.rex* looked
like from the outside.

NECK was thick
and strong.

SKULL held
powerful jaw with
sharp teeth.

ARMS were
short; hands had
clawed fingers.

HEADS UP! Herbivores, like this *Brachiosaurus*, were browsers. This means they chomped on leaves and other vegetation.

WHAT'S FOR DINNER?

inosaurs chose different kinds of food. They ate and digested it in different ways, too. About one-eighth of all dinosaurs were carnivores that ate small mammals, reptiles, and other dinosaurs. Most of the rest were herbivores, which ate plants. There were also a few insectivores, which ate bugs, and piscivores, which ate fish. Some dinosaurs were not choosy about their food and ate everything—small reptiles and mammals, insects, fish, and plants. These are called omnivores. (*Omni* means "all.")

Dinosaurs had different ways of eating. Each had the right teeth for its diet. Carnivores had long, sharp teeth, like a lion's. They used them to catch and rip up other animals. Carnivore teeth could tear off chunks of meat or the dinosaur could eat small animals whole.

Rounded, dull herbivore teeth stripped leaves off bark. Many plant-eating dinosaurs, such as **Styracosaurus** and *Triceratops*, had extra sets of teeth in their cheeks. These were used to grind the plants they ate into a mush that could be digested. But most dinosaur teeth and jaws were not designed for chewing. Instead, the food was swallowed in large chunks and broken down in the stomach.

Spinosaurus ate fish.

HERBIVORE TEETH VS CARNIVORE TEETH

Flat, dull teeth allowed herbivores to grind up the leaves and plants they ate.

Sharp, pointy teeth helped meat-eaters kill and rip apart other animals.

Plants have few calories, which are the units of energy in food. To get enough energy to keep their big bodies nourished, plant eaters had to spend most of their time eating.

Large herbivores needed a huge stomach to hold and break down all the plants they ate. Experts think most of these dinosaurs had a special chamber in their stomach. In this chamber, stomach acids would break down the plants. Then the nutrients could be absorbed.

When we think of meat-eating dinosaurs, we might imagine them constantly ripping other dinosaurs apart and eating them. It is true that carnivores attacked big herbivores and other carnivores. Some even ate others of their own species. But dinosaurs also ate small mammals, birds, and reptiles. We know this because fossilized remains of small animals have been found in the rib cages of meat-eating dinosaurs.

THE SCOOP ON POOP

Coprolite is a fancy word for poop fossil. Paleontologists have found many well-preserved piles of coprolites. By analyzing these poop fossils, they can tell if they came from herbivores or carnivores. They can learn a lot about the plant life of a certain time period by matching dinosaur skeletons to the types of plants in their poop.

Some plant eaters found a way to help their digestive system break down woody or tough plants. They swallowed small rocks called gastroliths. These rocks mashed up the food in their stomachs every time they moved. A few dinosaur skeletons have been found with these rocks in the place where the stomach would have been.

Fossilized dino poop

SLOW MOVER Kentrosaurus had a small head, a toothless beak for tearing leaves, and body armor for protection.

READY FOR BATTLE

Thyreophorans, also called armored dinosaurs, were among the first dinosaurs of the Early Jurassic Period. They were heavy, slow-moving herbivores. Some were just a few feet long. Others were almost 40 feet long. Thyreophorans had awesome protective body armor. Dinosaurs in one group, called stegosaurs, had bony plates running along their backs. Ankylosaurs were covered in bony plates that were raised, like large bumps, along their bodies. They all had small heads and tiny brains. They were not the smartest dinosaurs, but they were tough.

Thyreophoran fossils have been found on all seven continents, but they are most common in the western United States. There are 80 known thyreophorans. The name thyreophoran comes from Greek and means "shield bearer."

Many stegosaurs had two rows of spikes sticking out of their plates. Predators were less likely to attack stegosaurs since even sharp teeth couldn't bite the plates. All the stegosaurs walked on four feet. They had hard beaks that they used to snip leaves

Stegosaurus

and twigs off low-growing plants.

Stegosaurus is the best known of the stegosaur group. The protection of bony plates was important for a dinosaur that moved slowly and wasn't tough or intelligent. At up to 40 feet long, *Stegosaurus* was about ten times the size of a dog. But its brain was only one-quarter the size of a dog's brain.

Gigantspinosaurus

Gigantspinosaurus had two gigantic spines, or spikes, that stuck out of its shoulders. *Kentrosaurus* had bony plates on its neck and back, and two rows of spikes along its tail. Experts think the plates helped members of a herd identify each other. Their spiked tails, however, were excellent defensive weapons.

Ankylosaurs, also called armored lizards, were built like tanks and had fused (connected) bony plates all over their bodies. The earliest species, such as **Polacanthus** and **Nodosaurus**, were covered in light plates and thin spikes. *Nodosaurus* had a soft belly. It may have dropped down and hugged the ground to protect itself when attacked.

Minmi, another early kind of ankylosaur, was a nibbler. It bit off tiny parts of plants rather than swallowing them whole. Small bits of plants were found in the stomach of a well-preserved *Minmi* fossil.

Ankylosaurus, which evolved later in the Early Cretaceous Period, had a very heavy

Ankylosaurus

body on short, thick legs. *Ankylosaurus* weighed more than 8,000 pounds when fully grown. Even the biggest carnivores could not have tipped it over to get to its soft belly. And their big, sharp teeth wouldn't have been able to pierce the heavy armor.

FACT FILE: TAIL TALES

Thyreophorans' tails could be aimed at predators and used for attack.

Many stegosaurs had tails with four spikes arranged in a pattern. Tests with models of these spikes show that a tail like this would have been an effective weapon. *Stegosaurus* had the muscles to swing its tail hard at an attacker.

Stegosaurus

The club at the end of a young *Ankylosaurus*'s tail was as big and heavy as a bowling ball. As the dinosaur got older, the club would have grown even bigger. A hard thwack from that tail could have broken the bones of a predator.

Ankylosaurus

HEADWAY *Parasaurolophus* was named for the long, backward-facing crest on its head (*para* means "beside" and *lophos* means "crest" in Greek).

SPEED RACERS

rnithopods were not the biggest or the smartest or the most vicious dinosaurs. But they had several very useful features. Most could walk on either four feet or two feet, depending on whether they were eating or running. They were good at chewing and could get a lot of nutrition from their food. Some had duckbills for snipping plants and thumb spikes to gather food. Because of these advantages, ornithopods grew in size and in number.

The name ornithopod comes from two Greek words meaning "bird feet." Most of these dinosaurs had feet with three toes, like birds. There are 130 known ornithopods, and their fossils have been found everywhere in the world.

Ornithopods play a huge role in the history of fossil hunting. The first plant-eating dinosaur to be officially named was an ornithopod called *Iguanodon*. The first nests of dinosaur eggs found belonged to the ornithopod **Maiasaura**. The first nearly complete dinosaur skeleton ever found was another ornithopod, *Hadrosaurus*. It was found on a farm in Haddonfield, New Jersey, in 1858. The first fossilized dinosaur skin discovered was attached to the skeleton of an ornithopod called *Edmontosaurus*.

Ornithopods had interlocking rows of teeth. All those teeth allowed them to chew their food thoroughly. This meant they could break down tough plants for easier digestion and to get the most nutrients. As teeth wore down, new ones moved into their place.

Many ornithopods had thumb spikes. These were up to 6 inches long and very thick. The thumb spikes would have been good weapons against predators. Some scientists think they were most useful for breaking up fruit and gathering food, like a built-in knife.

Ornithopods could also walk on four

feet while eating, and then stand on two legs and run fast. Some, such as *Dryosaurus*, had strong legs that would have given it speed to escape predators.

Big, bulky *Iguanodon* had all the ornithopod advantages. It could switch from running on two legs to walking on four legs. It had many teeth to chew its food thoroughly. And it had big thumb spikes to do many jobs. The front of its beak was toothless, but it had 29 big teeth in each cheek. Its beak was sharp enough to snip off plants, and its cheeks were

Iguanodon

big enough to hold food while the teeth ground it up. *Iguanodon* also had a flexible pinkie finger to help it grab and gather food. These eating aids helped it grow to about 30 feet long and 9 feet tall. In fact, it was one of the biggest ornithopods. Using its size and its thumb spikes, it could survive fights with carnivores.

A group of ornithopods called hadrosaurs lived in the forests of

Europe, Asia, and North America in the Late Cretaceous Period. Their common name is duckbill, because the heads of some members resembled those of modern ducks. They had long, flat bills or short beaks that were just right for snipping twigs and leaves from trees.

Hadrosaurs were big, sturdy dinosaurs with all the helpful body parts of ornithopods. They also had horns, spikes, and crests. This headgear may have been only for show. But experts think it may have been used to attract mates or help the dinosaurs make louder sounds.

FACT FILE: SKIN AND BONES

In 1999, a 16-year-old amateur paleontologist named Tyler Lyson was searching for fossils on his uncle's farm in North Dakota. Lyson made an amazing discovery: a mummified Edmontosaurus skeleton. (Mummification is a process that dries and preserves skin.) The skeleton was almost whole, with the skin attached.

Lyson and a group of experts carefully dug up the skeleton. They named it "Dakota" and spent years studying it. The mummified skin showed bumps rather than scales. It may have had a striped pattern.

Lyson's discovery, on display at the North Dakota Heritage Center

MAKING A POINT *Styracosaurus* had four to six horns on its neck frill, one on each cheek, and one on its beak. It had short legs, and experts think it may have run up to 20 miles per hour.

CALL THEM "BIG HEADS"

They weren't known for their speed, size, or intelligence. But the dinosaur group called marginocephalians, or fringe heads, were definitely not ordinary. There were two kinds of dinosaurs in the group.

Horn-face dinosaurs, or ceratopsians, include *Triceratops* and its relatives. They had pointy horns all over their heads. Some also had sharp spikes sticking out and large frills that grew

Triceratops, a horn-faced dinosaur, had horns, frills, and ridges.

out of their skulls. Another group, called dome-heads, had thick caps of bone on their heads. All of the marginocephalian dinosaurs walked on four legs and they all ate plants.

Marginocephalian fossils have been found in Europe, Asia, and North America. There are 85 known marginocephalians.

These dinosaurs had other important features besides their horns. They had strong bodies and many teeth that were good for eating plants. Their tough beaks may have been covered in a hard protective coating called keratin, which is also found in human skin, hair, and nails.

When they were young, horn-face dinosaurs basically looked alike. Their horns changed shape and size as they grew older. Some horns vanished and others grew in. Adults had horns, frills, and spikes that were different from each other's.

Psittacosaurus was named for its head, which was like a parrot's (*psittakos* means "parrot" in Greek). It had teeth and a beak that could chop off plants.

Triceratops was one of the late arrivals on the dinosaur scene. It didn't appear until 69 million years ago—about 3 million years before all dinosaurs became extinct. It lived around the same time as *Tyrannosaurus rex*. Skeletons of both dinosaurs have been found with scars from battles between them. *Triceratops* was a big, heavy animal with a huge skull. How huge? Its head was about one-third the length of its whole body! Topping off its skull was an enormous frill, which pointed backward and extended up to 7 feet.

Paleontologists think the tight, bony domes of dome-head dinosaurs were used to butt one another in the sides when competing for mates.

Dome-head dinosaurs grew to only about 15 feet at their longest. They appeared in the Late Cretaceous Period. Mostly, they roamed western North America, as far east as New Mexico. Some have also been found in Asia.

Pachycephalosaurus had a bony skull that was more than 10 inches thick. Experts think it was used to head-butt rivals and predators. *Stegoceras* had large, forward-facing eye sockets. That may mean it had binocular vision, which helped it focus and know how far away something was.

Pachycephalosaurus

In **1971, two skeletons** were found in the Gobi Desert, their limbs locked in battle. They were a *Velociraptor* and a **Protoceratops**. Scientists think the two were fighting when a sandstorm killed them both. Although the fossils show the battle, we have to guess which dinosaur would have won.

Velociraptor was a theropod. It weighed about 40 pounds and was about 6 feet long. It had big, sharp claws and small, pointy teeth, and it moved quickly. Although it was not the most intelligent dinosaur, it was still pretty smart.

Protoceratops was a ceratopsian herbivore. It was about 6 feet long and weighed about 400 pounds. It had a small frill on its head and a hard beak. It was slow and had a very small brain.

It looks as though the *Protoceratops* has a grip on the *Velociraptor* in the illustration below. Which one do you think would have won the battle?

Protoceratops fighting a Velociraptor.

WHAT HAPPENED? A huge natural change wiped out the dinosaurs. Scientists are studying exactly what occurred.

AN END AND A BEGINNING

ntil 66 million years ago, dinosaurs wandered all over the planet. Big carnivores such as *T. rex* dominated. New species, including *Triceratops*, popped up. Then the fossil record shows they all became extinct. There is great debate about what kind of disaster killed the dinosaurs.

Most scientists think a huge asteroid from space hit Earth, creating tsunamis—giant tidal waves—and dust clouds.

Scientists have found a mineral called iridium in soil that dates back to the time of the dinosaur extinction. Iridium is rare on Earth, but there is plenty in asteroids. A truly massive asteroid could have wiped out the dinosaurs in just hours or days.

Another idea is that the end came over a long period of time. There is evidence that volcanoes were active around the time the dinosaurs disappeared. If volcanic activity was heavy throughout the world, smoke, ash, and gas could have blocked out the sun and cooled the climate. Much of the food supply for herbivores would have been destroyed. When the herbivores starved, carnivores would have lost their food supply and died, too.

When dinosaurs vanished, many small mammals survived. Scientists believe that because they were so small, they were able to live on very little food. They could have escaped heat by digging into the ground.

After the dinosaurs disappeared, mammals grew larger and larger. Giant forms of early elephants, tigers, bears, and whales lived between 66 million years ago and 10,000 years ago. Some of these huge mammals died out when the Ice Age reduced the amount of food available. Many were hunted by humans. But in many cases, they evolved into smaller animals that are still around today.

Mammoths were one of the biggest mammals. They are relatives of modern elephants. Mammoths had curved tusks and grew 7 to 14 feet tall. They died out around the end of the Ice Age.

Smilodon, the saber-toothed tiger, lived 2.5 million to 10,000 years ago. It hunted large herbivores and is known for its curved front teeth. Modern tigers are distant relatives of *Smilodon*.

As mammals grew bigger a new line of animal closely related to apes evolved around 6 million years ago. Over millions of years, this line evolved. As it evolved, it

Smilodon's curved front teeth were 11 inches long.

One humanlike species, *Homo habilis*, lived about 1.5 to 2.3 million years ago.

got smarter. It stood up straighter. We would have recognized it as being like us. These new animals had large, well-developed brains. They made tools and communicated. By 200,000 years ago this line evolved into modern humans, the same species as all of us, and by 60,000 years ago had begun spreading around the world.

THE SURVIVORS

Why did some animals survive when the dinosaurs died? When something huge changes in the environment, many animal species cannot survive. The survivors are able to live in conditions that killed off others. It might be because of what survivors eat, where they live, or how they are shaped.

Alligator gars

Tadpole shrimp

When the dinosaurs became extinct, most of the survivors lived in water. Survivors included great white sharks, alligator gars (fish with crocodile-shaped jaws), horseshoe crabs (which have blood that fights bacteria), and lamprey eels (which can attach their mouths to other fish and suck their blood).

Horseshoe crabs

Tuatara

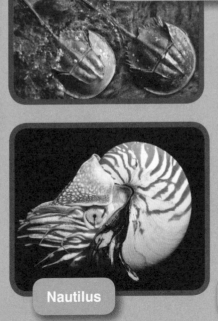

Nautilus

Great white shark

RESOURCES

Many museums and parks have dinosaur fossils on display. Some try to help visitors understand what the world was like in the Age of Dinosaurs. Some let you touch the bones. At a few, you can watch paleontologists at work.

MUSEUMS WITH DINOSAURS

American Museum of Natural History
New York, New York
www.amnh.org

Carnegie Museum of Natural History
Pittsburgh, Pennsylvania
www.carnegiemnh.org

Denver Museum of Nature & Science
Denver, Colorado
www.dmns.org

Dinosaur Discovery Museum
Kenosha, Wisconsin
www.kenosha.org/ wp-dinosaur

Dinosaur National Monument
Dinosaur, Colorado
www.nps.gov/dino

Dinosaur Provincial Park
Brooks, Alberta, Canada
www.albertaparks.ca/ dinosaur.aspx

Dinosaur State Park
Rocky Hill, Connecticut
www.dinosaurstatepark. org

Field Museum of Natural History
Chicago, Illinois
www.fieldmuseum.org

Natural History Museum of Los Angeles County
Los Angeles, California
www.nhm.org

Royal Tyrrell Museum
Drumheller, Alberta,
Canada
www.tyrrellmuseum.com

Science Museum of
Minnesota
St. Paul, Minnesota
www.smm.org

Wyoming
Dinosaur Center
Thermopolis,
Wyoming
www.wyodino.org

Yale Peabody Museum of
Natural History
New Haven, Connecticut
www.peabody.yale.edu

BOOKS

Boy, Were We Wrong About Dinosaurs!, by Kathleen V.
Kudlinski (Frances Lincoln Children's Books)

*Digging Dinosaurs: The Search That Unraveled the
Mystery of Baby Dinosaurs*, by John R. Horner and
James Gorman (Perennial Library)

*Discovery Dinopedia: The Complete Guide to
Everything Dinosaur*, by the Discovery Channel
(Discovery/Time)

WEBSITES TO CHECK OUT

DinoBuzz from University of California Museum of
Paleontology
www.ucmp.berkeley.edu/diapsids/dinobuzz.html

Dinosaurs from Discovery Kids
www.discoverykids.com/category/dinosaurs

Zoom Dinosaurs from Enchanted Learning
www.enchantedlearning.com/subjects/dinosaurs

DINOSAUR PRONUNCIATION GUIDE

Allosaurus (al-oh-SORE-us)

Anhanguera (ahn-han-GAIR-ah)

Ankylosaurus (an-ky-loh-SORE-us)

Apatosaurus (uh-PA-toh-sore-us)

Archaeopteryx (ar-kee-OP-tur-iks)

Argentinosaurus (ahr-jen-TEE-noh-sore-us)

Brachiosaurus (BRA-key-oh-sore-us)

Brontosaurus (bron-tuh-SORE-us)

Camarasaurus (KAM-a-rah-sore-us)

Carcharodontosaurus (car-ca-roh-DON-tih-sore-us)

Coelophysis (see-lo-FIE-sis)

Deinonychus (dy-NAH-nih-kus)

Dilophosaurus (die-loh-foe-SORE-us)

Diplodocus (dih-PLAH-duh-kuss)

Drinker (DRIN-kur)

Dryosaurus (DRY-oh-sore-us)

Edmontosaurus (ed-MAHN-toh-sore-us)

Eoraptor (EE-oh-rap-tore)

Gigantoraptor (JY-gant-oh-rap-tore)

Gigantspinosaurus (JY-gant-spy-noh-sore-us)

Hadrosaurus (hay-droh-SORE-us)

Herrerasaurus (huh-rare-uh-SORE-us)

Iguanodon (ih-GWA-noh-don)

Kentrosaurus (KEN-troh-SORE-us)

Maiasaura (my-ya-SORE-a)

Massospondylus (mas-oh-SPON-dih-lus)

Minmi (MIN-mee)

Nodosaurus (NO-doh-sore-us)

Ornithomimus (or-nih-thoh-MY-mus)

Oviraptor (OH-vih-rap-tore)

Pachycephalosaurus (pak-ih-seff-uh-loh-SORE-us)

Parasaurolophus (PAR-ah-sore-ah-loh-fuss)

Polacanthus (pol-uh-KAN-thuss)

Protoceratops (proh-toh-SERR-a-tops)

Psittacosaurus (sit-ah-koh-SORE-us)

Qianzhousaurus (key-an-shoo-SORE-us)

Quetzalcoatlus (kwet-sal-KOH-at-lus)

Spinosaurus (SPY-no-sore-us)

Stegoceras (steh-go-SAIR-us)

Stegosaurus (STEH-go-sore-us)

Styracosaurus (sty-RAK-oh-sore-us)

Tawa (TAH-wah)

Therizinosaurus (theh-rih-ZEE-noh-sore-us

Triceratops (try-SERR-a-tops)

Troodon (TROH-uh-don)

Tyrannosaurus (tie-RAN-oh-sore-us)

Velociraptor (vuh-LAH-si-rap-tore)

Vulcanodon (vull-KAN-uh-don)

Yangchuanosaurus (YANG-shwan-oh-sore-us)

Zhenyuanlong suni (jen-HWAN-long SOO-nee)

Zuniceratops (zoo-nee-SERR-a-tops)

INDEX

Illustrations are indicated by **boldface**. When they fall within a page span, the entire span is **boldface**.

CREDITS AND ACKNOWLEDGMENTS

Writer Lori Stein
Produced by Scout Books & Media Inc
President and Project Director Susan Knopf
Project Manager Brittany Gialanella
Copyeditor Beth Adelman, Michael Centore
Proofreader Chelsea Burris
Designer Annemarie Redmond
Advisors Michael Rentz, PhD, *Lecturer in Mammology, Iowa State University;* Dr. Joseph Sertich, *Curator of Vertebrate Paleontology, Denver Museum of Nature and Science*

Thanks to the Time Inc. Books team: Margot Schupf, Anja Schmidt, Beth Sutinis, Deirdre Langeland, Georgia Morrissey, Megan Pearlman, Melodie George, and Sue Chodakiewicz.

Special thanks to the Discovery and Animal Planet Creative and Licensing Teams: Denny Chen, Tracy Conner, Elizabeta Ealy, Robert Marick, Doris Miller, Sue Perez-Jackson, and Janet Tsuei.

PHOTO CREDITS

Key: SS – Shutterstock; DT – Dreamstime; GY – Getty; NPL – naturepl.com; IS – iStock
TtB: Top to bottom; LtR: Left to right; CL: Clockwise from top left
FRONT COVER: ©DM7/SS
p. 1: ©DM7/SS; p. 3: ©Discovery Communications, LLC; p. 4: ©Leonello Calvetti/DT; p. 9 ©CoreyFord/IS; p. 10 TtB: ©Freerlaw/DT, ©CoreyFord/IS; p. 11 TtB: ©CoreyFord/IS, ©leonello/IS; p. 15 TtB LtR: ©Viktorya170377/SS, ©Catmando/SS, ©Sofia Santos/SS, ©Viktorya170377/SS, ©Kostyantyn Ivanyshen/SS, ©Viktorya170377/SS, ©Anna Rassadnikova/SS; p. 16: ©estt/IS; p. 21 TtB: ©CoreyFord/IS, ©homeworks255/IS; pp. 22-23: ©Catmando/SS; pp. 24-25: ©Elenarts/SS; pp. 26-27 LtR: ©Mr1805/DT, ©By Tim Evanson from Washington, D.C., United States of America [CC BY-SA 2.0 (http://creativecommons.org/licenses/by-sa/2.0/)], via Wikimedia Commons; p. 28: ©DM7/SS; p. 34: ©Boborsillo/DT; p. 37: ©Stock Connection/Stock Connection/Superstock; p. 38: ©BBC/Discovery Communications, LLC; p. 43: ©Dan Porges/GY; pp. 44-45: ©Catmando/SS; p. 46: ©Catmando/SS; pp. 48-49: ©Discovery Communications, LLC; p. 51 TtB: ©Aunt_Spray/IS, ©danefromspain/IS, ©apiguide/SS; pp. 52-53: ©MR1805/IS; p. 54: ©Elenarts/IS; pp. 56-57: ©Discovery Communciations, LLC; p. 60: ©Anadolu Agency/GY; p. 63: ©By Ghedoghedo (Own work) [CC BY-SA 3.0 (http://creativecommons.org/licenses/by-sa/3.0/)], via Wikimedia Commons; pp. 64-65 TtB: ©Sofia Santos, ©leonello/IS; p. 66: ©Catmando/SS; p. 69: ©Elenarts/SS; p. 70 LtR: ©Ken Backer/DT, ©MarquesPhotography/IS; pp. 72-73 LtR: ©farbled/SS, ©By Poozeum (Own work) [CC BY-SA 4.0 (http://creativecommons.org/licenses/by-sa/4.0/)], via Wikimedia Commons, ©By Poozeum (Own work) [CC BY-SA 4.0 (http://creativecommons.org/licenses/by-sa/4.0/)], via Wikimedia Commons, ©By Poozeum (Own work) [CC BY-SA 4.0 (http://creativecommons.org/licenses/by-sa/4.0/)], via Wikimedia Commons; p. 74: ©Elenarts/IS; p. 77: ©BBC/Discovery Communications, LLC; pp. 78-79: ©CoreyFord/IS; pp. 82-83 LtR: ©Herschel Hoffmeyer/SS, ©Linda Bucklin/SS; p. 84: ©Filippo onez Vanzo/SS; pp. 88-89: ©Dariush M/SS; pp. 90-91 LtR: ©CoreyFord/IS, ©WILL KINCAID/ASSOCIATED PRESS; p. 92: ©MR1805/IS; p. 94: ©Elenarts/IS; p. 97: ©By Credit to - user Ballista from the English wikipedia. (Own work) [GFDL (http://www.gnu.org/copyleft/fdl.html) or CC-BY-SA-3.0 (http://creativecommons.org/licenses/by-sa/3.0/)], via Wikimedia Commons; p. 99: ©AP Photo/Stocktrek Images; p. 100: ©Elenarts/IS; p. 104-105 LtR: ©Sasha Samardzija/SS, ©Michael Rosskothen/SS; p. 106 LtR: ©crazystocker/SS, ©Dirk Ercken/SS; p. 107 CL: ©Wasu Watcharadachaphong/SS, ©Rudmer Zwerver/SS, ©davidpstephens/SS, ©bluehand/SS.